SCOTT PACK

How to Perfect Your Submission

Contents

Introduction 1

Before You Send Anything 3

Are you ready? 3

Research 5

Strategy 9

The Submission 12

Query Letter 14

Classic Mistakes 16

The Pitch 18

Synopsis 19

Sample Chapters 23

Non-Fiction Book Proposal 25

Follow Up 29

Success 31

Some Positive Thoughts 34

Conclusion 35

FAQs 37

Appendix 1: Query Letter Template 44

Appendix 2: Contact Details 46

Acknowledgements 47

'Scott is the rarest of one-two punches, having a wonderful understanding of both the creative and business sides of the publishing industry. If I could give you one bit of advice, it'd be to shut up and listen to everything he has to say. If I could give you two bits of advice, it'd be that plus people getting punched in the groin is never not funny.' **Caimh McDonnell, bestselling author of *The Dublin Trilogy***

'Scott has championed me from the very start of my self-published writing career. In 2011 he quoted that I was as good, if not better, than any traditionally published romcom author. As I sit at #1 in the Kindle bestselling chart, I guess he knows what he's talking about.' **Nicola May, No1 best-selling author of *The Corner Shop in Cockleberry Bay***

'Scott knows the publishing industry inside-out and whenever I work with him, I know my authors are in good hands.' **Charlotte Seymour, literary agent**

'Few people in the publishing world can claim to have such wide and varied knowledge and experience of so many aspects of the industry. As a publisher, bookseller, author and speaker (not necessarily in that order), Scott not only has the breadth and depth of experience to impart but he does so forthrightly and with great humour. I wouldn't trust anyone else to give me advice, he really knows his stuff!' **Valerie Brandes, founder, Jacaranda Books**

'Scott has unrivalled experience as a book buyer, editor and publisher; he's seen and done it all from across the business. If you want to know about any aspect of the book world, what he says really does matter and will make a huge difference.' **Michael Bhaskar, co-founder and publishing director, Canelo**

'Scott is a rare beast who combines pragmatic commerciality with creative flair and sensitivity, all wrapped in a no BS, tell-it-how-it-is persona. His short cuts on how to win are invaluable guides not only on how to get published but also how to sell books. Unfortunately if he thinks your magnum opus is crap he will happily tell you so.' **David Roche, former Chief Executive, Borders UK & Ireland**

'Not only is Scott Pack the best editor I've worked with, but as a publisher, he's erudite, passionate and creative – must-have qualities every successful publisher should combine.' **Ray Robinson, author of *Electricity* and *The Mating Habits of Stags***

'From being the key national bookseller at Waterstones to becoming a publisher and champion of digital publishing, the inveterate enthusiast Scott Pack has long been a highly regarded and influential figure in the book trade.' **Charley Viney, The Viney Shaw Agency**

'Scott is truly wise about all aspects of the publishing process

v

and industry. He's also a tiny bit irreverent, which means he will always tell it how it is.' **Abi Silver, author of the Burton & Lamb crime series**

'Scott is known in the publishing industry for his straight-talking approach – he can be relied upon for sensible and honest advice.' **Angus Phillips, director, Oxford International Centre for Publishing**

'I had the pleasure of working with Scott at HarperCollins and I learned a huge amount from him. As well as possessing a deep understanding of the business of publishing books, he is also forward-thinking and knows exactly how latest innovations can impact his work effectively. Scott brings a hell of a lot to the party.' **Sam Missingham, founder, Lounge Marketing**

Introduction

Since 2015, I have taught a number of classes at the offices of the *Guardian* newspaper in London as part of the *Guardian Masterclass* series, in which experts in certain fields pass on their knowledge to a fee-paying audience. My classes were advertised under a few different names but the basic theme was the same for each of them: How to pitch your manuscript to an agent or publisher.

I have spent nearly twenty years working in the book world, most of them as a publisher, and I have had thousands of manuscripts submitted to me during that time. It never ceases to amaze me how many otherwise intelligent, articulate and sensible people make a complete hash of this process and I see the same mistakes made over and over again.

My *Guardian Masterclass* was designed to with two aims in mind. First, to ensure that the attendees did not make any of those mistakes. Second, to give them the tools they needed to prepare the most professional submission possible. If they listened to my advice then they stood an excellent chance of getting their work read and seriously considered by agents and publishers.

This short book distills those three-hour classes into what should be a fairly quick read, no more than half an hour or so. Although you won't have the pleasure of my dynamic presentation style and quick wit, you will have all the information you need to make sure your submission is as strong as possible. I know that several writers who attended my classes have gone on to be signed up by agents and publishers and some already have their books in print, so I hope this works for you.

Since first publishing this short book I have written a much longer book called *Tips from a Publisher*. It explores many aspects of the book world and includes lots of practical writing advice. It is available, as they say, from all good bookshops.

Before You Send Anything

Are you ready?

Before you take one step further on your quest to get published it is important that you pause for a moment, take a deep breath and work out if you really want all this hassle.

Take a cold hard look at yourself. What you are about to do is bloody hard. What lies ahead for most of you is months, perhaps years of frustration. It can dent your confidence. It can crush your self-esteem. Your dream may never come true. This can be a soul-destroying experience. Do you have what it takes to get through this? If in doubt, consider other routes such as privately publishing, or self-publishing. Or even not publishing at all. This process isn't just about how good your book is, it is about how much you want to be a published author and whether or not you are prepared to deal with everything that comes with that. You do not have to go down this road and there is no shame in opting out at any stage.

What are you trying to achieve? The approach you should

take with your submission will differ depending on your hopes and aspirations. If you genuinely believe your work of genius will sell for a million-pound advance then it is pointless approaching smaller agencies or independent publishers. If you have written a technical journal that only one or two specialist publishers would ever be interested in then you are better off approaching them directly and may not need an agent at all. It is worth spending some time thinking about what it is you are trying to achieve and developing a plan to help make that happen.

Who has read your book? I would urge you not to submit your book until it has been read by at least a small number of qualified people who have offered feedback. People who are not qualified to do this include relatives, loved ones, people you are sleeping with, people you want to sleep with, people you have slept with in the past, people you may want to sleep with in the future. These people, no matter how honest they are in real life, will generally not want to ~~tell you your book is shit~~ point out your book's flaws for all sorts of reasons. Ideally you would find someone who knows a good book when they read one, is blunt and direct, has no agenda and would be prepared to spend the time reading your work and making a few notes. The most opinionated person in your book group wouldn't be a bad person to start with.

Is it really ready to send out? The majority of manuscripts I reject are clearly a couple of drafts short of being ready. Another few months, a bit more work, and they may have stood more chance of making it to the next stage. Often when I offer feedback on a manuscript the author replies with 'I knew that section wasn't quite right, thanks for confirming it for me' or something like that. If they already knew this, why are they submitting for publication? Agents and publishers do not expect your work to be perfect and ready to publish but why not increase your chances by at least getting it to the point where you genuinely think it is as good as it can be, and your advance readers agree?

Can you handle rejection? The vast majority of you are going to be rejected more than once, perhaps dozens of times. Get used to it. It isn't nice, though, and it can really knock your confidence. How good are you at receiving criticism? You may be surprised by how hard you take a rejection. However philosophical or thick-skinned you may think you are, your 25th rejection for the same book may be one too many. It has happened to a lot of great writers, you may be another of them. Can you hack it?

* * *

Research

One of the top complaints from agents and publishers about the submissions they receive is lack of research: authors not doing some simple groundwork before submitting. Here are some things you can do to avoid being that person.

Trade press. Spend time getting to know the industry you are attempting to enter. If you are successful then you are effectively taking on a new job, a new career, even if only part-time, so do the same sort of research you would when going for a big job interview. If you are in the UK then read *The Bookseller* magazine, the main trade publication, which is available in print and online editions. In the US you would want to concentrate on *Publishers Weekly*. But check out the rest of the trade press online too. Follow these publications on Twitter or join their pages on Facebook. Do the same with their key journalists. Over time you will learn who the up-and-coming agents, editors and publishers are, who represents or publishes whom, what books have sold for big advances. Understanding the mood of the industry, what appears to be working and what isn't working, will prove helpful in your quest to become a published author yourself.

Agent and publisher websites. If an agent or publisher would welcome your submission then it will say as much on their website. If they are not going out of their way to tell you this then they probably don't want to hear from you. Their website will also hopefully tell you about the authors they represent or publish, who their key staff are, etc. They don't take too long to navigate and you can learn a lot from them.

Acknowledgements pages. When looking for ideas as to where to send your manuscript, the Thank Yous at the beginning or end of published books can be a good start. Most authors will thank their editors (sometimes tricky people to pin down online) and agents. An hour spent browsing through your own bookshelves and jotting down names will be an hour well spent.

Who represents the authors you admire? This is an extension of the previous point but is still worth making. If you consider Author X to be an influence on your work, why not try submitting to their agent? If the agent likes *their* work they might like yours too. A few words of caution, however: if your work is derivative of, or very similar to, Author X then I would not advise this route. Agents don't want copycat authors. Something with the same tone, style or sensibilities is fine, an imitation is not.

Hang out on Twitter. Lots of agents, publishing houses, editors and other publishing professionals are online these days and Twitter is a great way to, quite legitimately, hang out with them and find out what they have to say. Sure, they'll spend lots of time plugging their books and cooing over cute photos of cats, but they will also offer insight into their work. Feel free to interact with them but don't become a stalker. No one likes stalkers. Not even other stalkers. At my classes, when I ask for a show of hands from people who use Twitter, usually only about half of the attendees put their hands up. Now, there are lots of great reasons *not* to be on Twitter, and I would love to use it less myself, but it is undoubtedly a place where the people who might end up publishing your book are hanging out on a daily basis so if you are not there amongst them then you are probably at a disadvantage.

Writers' & Artists' Yearbook. This classic resource is well worth purchasing as it contains contact details for pretty much every agent and publishing imprint that matters as well as heaps of extra content and essays on all manner of issues relating to the book world. For several years it contained a piece by me all about blogs but then blogs stopped being interesting and they took it out, but now it has an article I wrote about the mathematics of publishing, the numbers behind the scenes in the book world. It is also a tax deductible expense, so that's nice. The US equivalent is the annual *Writer's Market* publication.

Writers' communities. There is a plethora of online writing forums and communities. Sure, there are lots of trolls and arseholes to be found lurking within them, and cliques of writers can sometimes form and be hard to crack but, in the main, they are useful places to discuss your work. Do spend some time checking them out before diving in, as some will be better suited to your personality and writing style. There are also, of course, many writing groups in the real world but these do involve having to talk to actual people.

Workshops and festivals. Hardly a week goes by without some literary festival in Upper Throtting, or somewhere similar. Not only that, lots of them have workshops, opportunities to hear agents and publishing folk talk about the industry and other useful content over and above the usual authors droning on about their books. Check out the programmes of festivals near you and see what's occurring. There are also several writer-focused events and many of these will have one-to-one sessions that can be booked with editors and agents. These are, I think, a worthwhile investment of time and money.

* * *

Strategy

OK, so you've done your research. Now you need to spend some time planning how you are going to approach the submissions process. If you find an agent then, from that point on, your work will be subject to a strategy at every stage of its life – when your agent submits it to publishers, when your editor pitches it to their publishing team, when the sales department sells the book to retailers, when the marketing and publicity people try to get reviews and media coverage – so you might as well start now.

Create a longlist. While conducting your research you should keep an ongoing list of all the agents and/or publishers you think would be good matches for your book. It is best to do this as you go along and add notes to remind you why they are on the list and about their specific submission requirements. I am a big fan of using a spreadsheet for this process as this can evolve to keep track of your submissions and responses once you start sending your work out there.

Sort into priority order. Once you are happy that you have researched yourself to tears then you can sort your list into priority order. Who is your dream agent, the one you would go with if everyone you sent your work to offered you a contract? They go top of the list. Work your way down from there. This is an important step, especially if you are thinking positively, as you want to give your dream outcome a chance of actually happening. I know of one author who avoided sending his work to his ideal agent as he didn't want to send it to them 'too early'.

He ended up getting an offer from one of the other agents and found himself with the dilemma of whether to accept the offer, hold off that agent while he tried his ideal agent, or decline the offer and hope his dream agent came through later. OK, so not the worst situation to be in, but a bit messy and best avoided. If you have done your research and made sure your submission is ready then there is no problem approaching your favoured agent first.

Identify your top five or six. It makes sense to send out more than one submission at a time. Agents expect this and do not mind. I would suggest five or six at a time is about right as it spreads your bets to a degree while also keeping things at a manageable level. Rank your entire list so that you are prepared for the next round of submissions if required.

More research on each. Now to concentrate on your top group. No matter how much research you have done to date, do some more. If you haven't read at least two books represented by each agent, or published by each editor/publisher, then do it now. Check their Twitter feeds. If an opportunity to interact comes up, take it but don't be a weirdo. Find out what books they have sold or acquired recently, take note if they are having a particularly busy time, keep an extra special eye out for any moans or complaints they have. Sense check your decision. If you need to call someone sobbing at midnight because you can't get the ending of your second book right, is this the person you'd want to call?

Personalise approach. Think about what you want to say to each of the five people on your list. It needs to be different for each. You are not sending out a circular or round robin letter. If you don't have two or three great reasons for sending to that person then they should not be on the list.

Submit. Now you are ready to pull together your submission. Don't even think of sending stuff out until you have addressed all of the above. I mean it.

The Submission

And now to the submission package itself. These days most agents will accept submissions via email. They will be expecting the following for a fiction submission:

A query letter. We tend to refer to the introductory message that accompanies a submission as a query letter, or cover letter, even though these days, of course, it will usually take the form of an email.

A pitch. A paragraph or two within the query letter or email that tells the recipient what the book is about and, hopefully, gets them excited about it.

A synopsis. A one-page summary of the book and the key plot.

Sample chapters. Usually three sample chapters or a portion from the start of the book.

However, things are slightly different for a non-fiction submission. You still need a query letter containing a pitch, and a sample of your writing, but instead of a synopsis you would include:

Book Proposal. A page or two that explains the rationale behind the book, why you are the person to write it and who you think the audience might be.

Chapter Breakdown. A brief summary of the book, chapter by chapter.

Over the coming pages I look at each of the above elements in more detail but before I do, I need to impart probably the most important piece of advice in this entire book…

READ THE BLOODY GUIDELINES!

Every publisher or agent who welcomes submissions will have some form of guidelines on their website. Read them. Read them and follow them. I would estimate that 30-40% of all the submissions I have ever received ignored one or more of the guidelines. If they want to see three chapters, do not send them four. If they want the first 5,000 words, don't send them 6,000, or 1,000! If they specify a format, font or template, then use it. If your submission does not get read because you ignored submission guidelines then you only have yourself to blame.

Think about it. The guidelines are there because the person receiving your submission gets hundreds, if not thousands, such submissions every year. Going through them is a mammoth task. They are asking you, politely, to follow certain rules in order to make that process easier for them. Why would you then deliberately ignore that request and make it harder for them? And if you do that, do you really expect them to look upon you and your work kindly?

* * *

Query Letter

Does the ideal query letter exist?

Accepting that every agent and publisher is different and will have different requirements, like and dislikes, there probably isn't one truly perfect query letter, but you can write one that avoids all the mistakes that drive agents up the wall, and that's a bloody good start. Of course, these days they are query emails, rather than letters, but you get the idea.

Intro. This needs to be personal. *Dear Scott*, for example. *Dear Sirs* (it does happen) is impersonal and ignores the fact that men are in the minority in this industry. More than one of my female friends who are agents and publishers will not read past *Dear Sirs* if they receive an email addressed in that fashion, and rightly so.

About your book. Open with some brief information about your book. 'I am seeking representation for my crime novel, *Where Evil Remains*, which is complete at 85,000 words' is all you need.

Why are you sending it? Explain why you are sending it to this individual. Don't go over the top with flattery, just be honest. There is a reason you have selected them, so tell them. Unless that reason is 'you are the only agent left who hasn't rejected me' in which case I suggest you lie.

The pitch. This is a brief, one paragraph blurb for your book. It is probably the most important part of your cover letter so there is more detail on this later.

Comparison. It can help the agent if you are able to compare your book to recent or well-known books to give them an idea of the sort of thing you are sending them. Doing this without sounding like you are bragging is a good idea.

A bit about you. Agents and publishers do not care if you are married, or whether or not you have kids. They couldn't give a toss about your extensive record collection, love of knitting or your great sense of humour (unless you are pitching a book about the history of vinyl records or guerrilla knitting). Give them basic and relevant information. 'I am a 34-year-old English teacher who works as a police community support officer in my spare time' does the job perfectly (he can probably write OK, he knows a bit about how the policing system works!)

Keep it to one page. There is no query letter that needs to be more than one page long, or the equivalent if we are talking about an email. I don't care if you disagree.

That's it. That really is it. Nothing else is required in your cover letter. No jokes, no banter, no rambling, nothing.

At the end of this ebook you will find a template for the 'ideal' query letter which you are very free to copy and adapt for your own use.

* * *

Classic Mistakes

It is easy to make mistakes but it is even easier to avoid them by not being an idiot. Here are some classic mistakes that idiots make all the time.

Spelling the name wrong. My name is Scott, with two Ts. My surname is Pack. Not Park. Or Packer. There are only nine letters in my name, if you can't get them right then I am willing to bet a year's salary that your book is not going to be good enough to get published. Check and double check the spelling of the name of your recipient. It's just polite.

Typos. Computers are wonderful inventions and they all have this splendid spellchecking function. Please use it. Check your cover letter, synopsis and sample chapters for spelling mistakes. Then get someone else to check them. Agents and publishers won't get too upset if the odd typo sneaks in but some submissions are riddled with them, which is just plain sloppy.

Outrageous claims. Your book is not going to sell as well as *Harry Potter*, I can tell you that now, so don't bother claiming it will. Your book is not as good as *Catch-22*, either, so don't make comparisons. What we care about is your story and how well you've written it, not the size of your cojones. Big, bold, outrageous claims suggest an author with either a) unrealistic expectations or b) a massive ego. Both types of authors are best avoided. Of course, once an author has been successfully published and has a few bestsellers under their belt the chances are that they'll develop a massive ego and have unrealistic expectations, bless them, but you are not there yet.

Genres that don't exist. Can I make it clear now that there is no such thing as a 'fiction novel'. I receive several submissions every year for 'fiction novels'. There *is* such a thing as 'an author who doesn't know what they are talking about' though. Best not define your book as 'unclassifiable' or 'genre-busting' either. Also, a book cannot be a 'crossover hit' until it has been published in one category and then crossed over to another. Think about the departments and sections of a bookshop. Where would your book go? Just call it that.

Rambling nonsense. Keep things brief, polite and personal. Do not ramble on. Do not give us a reason to sigh and regret opening up the email. Do not give us an excuse not to read your synopsis.

Quirky. You may well be hilarious. Your friends and family may think you are hilarious. You may even have written a hilarious book. You do not need to write a hilarious query letter. Funny and quirky are annoying 99% of the time when it comes to submissions. Do not risk it. Also, do not enclose or attach anything other than the requested or required content. No glitter – it has happened.

* * *

The Pitch

It could be argued that the pitch is the most important part of your submission. It is the first sight the agent or publisher will get of your story, and it is the story that really matters.

One paragraph. The pitch should take up one paragraph of your cover letter. Any more and you'll struggle to keep your letter to a single page. You could stretch to two if you were really disciplined about length but do avoid the temptation to witter on too much.

Summarise the book in under 100 words. Here's a tip. Try summarising a few classic books, or some of your favourite books, in no more than 50 words. It can be done and is great practice for your own pitch. The word count is not a strict rule, by any means, but is a good target to aim for. If you exceed 100 words when pitching your book then you are not pitching it efficiently. Brevity is good at this juncture.

Think of it like a cover blurb. This is not a synopsis. You do not have to fit everything in. You need to make someone want to read your book in just the same way as publishers use the back cover blurb. Thankfully, this is really easy to research, just pick up any paperback book and see how it is done. Find some books that are similar in style, scope or potential audience to yours and copy out their blurbs. Actually type them up word for word. You'll find this an excellent way to analyse how it is done, get a feel for the format and tone, and try to replicate that for your pitch.

This is your elevator pitch. It's a clichéd scenario but it works. Imagine you are sharing an elevator ride with an agent/publisher/film producer and you have 30 seconds in which to pitch your story. What can you say to ensure they want to keep the conversation going when the elevator doors open? Stick that down in your pitch.

* * *

Synopsis

Writing a synopsis is not easy and requires a different set of skills to writing a novel, or even a pitch. It is one of the most difficult parts of the process and is a common stumbling block with submissions. But don't get in too much of a panic about it. Hardly anyone can write a good synopsis, and agents and publishers know that. This is not an excuse to be sloppy, however, and what follows are some tips to help you create the best synopsis you can.

What a synopsis isn't

A cover blurb. You've already done the cover blurb thing with your pitch, you don't need to do it again, only longer.

A novella. This isn't a cut down version of your book. It is a summary of it. It needs to be short.

A summary of every plot and sub-plot. In order to write a synopsis you will need to leave a lot of stuff out, and that may well mean dropping sub-plots or sections of the book that are not immediately relevant to the central plot.

Spoiler-free. Please do not worry about revealing the twist, or the ending, or the secret identity. The synopsis needs to contain the whole plot, from start to finish, spoilers and all.

More than 500 words. I have spoken with some agents who feel that anything over 300 words is superfluous but a maximum of 500 is going to be acceptable to pretty much everyone. Any more and you are pushing your luck. Don't say I didn't warn you. However, do remember my mantra of reading the guidelines. Occasionally an agent will request a longer synopsis, in which case you may have more room to play with.

More than a page long. In general, though, if your synopsis is longer than a page in normal font then it is probably too long. I don't care if you think you need an extra paragraph. You are wrong. Again, consider the poor recipient. Do you think they prefer receiving a concise, 500-word synopsis that does a great job of summarising the plot, or a four-page one?

What a synopsis is

A simple summary of the plot. That's all it is. A summary of what happens in the book, leaving out anything that distracts from the central plot. Your pitch can be colourful and emotive and work as a piece of advertising. Your synopsis is cold and direct and functional. Writing it will probably do your head in.

Straightforward. If your synopsis is confusing, when it is intended as a simple summary, then the assumption will be that your book is confusing. Avoid convoluted backtracking or introducing surprise elements.

Unemotional. All your lyricism and emotion can go into the book itself, there is no room for these things in a synopsis. Strip out any emotive language, any attempts to drive pace or write poetic sentences. Keep it simple. It may seem dull but it needs to do a specific job for you.

The One-Sentence Synopsis

If you find yourself struggling to write your synopsis, and especially if you are finding it hard to keep it to one page, here's one method that may help as it forces you to be ruthless to start with and cut things right back to the bare bones before gradually building it back up.

Summarise your book in one sentence. If you absolutely had to explain your book in no more than one sentence, how would you do it? This will cut through to the very essence of your book, removing any excess baggage.

Expand that to 50 words. Now, add a few more words or sentences to flesh out your summary. 50 words is not a lot, though, so you'll have to be frugal. What you are left with should be a really concise, tight, simply summary of your book.

Now increase to 250 words. OK, now you can elaborate a bit and fill in the gaps. Do everything you can to fit your entire plot into this space.

Do you need more? How successful have you been? If you have done the job then stop right there, you really don't need to go on.

One last go, but keep it under 500. If you absolutely must add some more detail then do so but go over 500 words at your peril.

The Bullet Point Synopsis

Here's another method to try if you are finding this synopsis shizzle hard.

Create bullet points. Try to summarise the plot in 10 one-sentence bullet points. Keep them short and, of course, in chronological order.

Use this as a framework. If you've done a half-decent job then you now have the bones of a synopsis. Time to put some flesh on them.

Expand each point. Add more detail, perhaps another sentence or two, to each bullet point.

Now get rid of those bloody bullet points. Delete the bullets, merge the sentences and tweak as needed to make it flow as one document.

* * *

Sample Chapters

As mentioned already, every publisher and agent will have guidelines for what sort of material they want to see and how they want it presented, so I am not going to pre-empt or second guess that here. What I am going to do is give you a simple checklist that is well worth running through.

You'd be surprised (or maybe not, now that you have read this far) how many authors prepare really strong cover letters, synopses and pitch packages but let themselves down with a poorly-presented sample of work.

Do this stuff, and it shouldn't happen to you:

Follow the guidelines. I know, I know, I have said this before but it bears repeating. What sample content has the agent or publisher asked for? If three chapters, then send them three chapters. If 10,000 words, then send them 10,000 words. Apart from clear exceptions – your first three chapters are only 50 words in total, your book is only 9,000 words long – you need to do as you are told. And if you are an exception then check with the agent first and see what they want you to do.

Format correctly. Nearly all agents will want you to send your sample chapters as a Microsoft Word document. If you use different word processing software then you may need to export your work as a Word file. If you are doing that then check that it opens correctly and looks OK on someone else's computer before sending it in as part of the submission. I tend to read my submissions on my Kindle, and Word documents are far easier to read on that device than PDFs as the former are more flexible and can be viewed at any font size. Worth bearing in mind if you were thinking of sending in PDF format. If in doubt, go for Times New Roman as your font and format the document so that the lines are double-spaced.

Check for typos. Agents and publishers aren't too worried by the occasional spelling error, but a manuscript littered with them just seems sloppy and doesn't show your work in the best light. Ideally you would get someone else to read over your work and check for any spelling, grammar or punctuation errors before you send it out. A second pair of eyes can be useful because you may well have become 'blind' to your own errors at this stage, having written and read through all the content several times.

Adverb alert. A classic sign of an 'amateur' writer is overuse of adjectives and particularly adverbs. This ebook isn't intended to address any issues with your writing style, it is designed to help you perfect your submission, but I am throwing in this one writing tip anyway, because it is a common issue with the manuscripts I am sent. Count the number of adverbs in your opening few pages. If you hit double figures then alarm bells should be ringing. I often say to authors I am working with that if they had to do ten push-ups every time they used an adverb then they'd soon stop using them so often.

* * *

Non-Fiction Book Proposal

If you are submitting a non-fiction title such as a history book, science book or biography, then you may be doing so before the book is completed. This is not unusual for non-fiction, although it is actively discouraged for novels. As always, I will refer you to the agent or publisher guidelines, but if you are a leading expert on Victorian architecture and want to write a book about it then it would be acceptable to pitch the concept to an agent or publisher before going off and doing all the research and writing.

In this situation, you would still be expected to provide a query letter containing a pitch but instead of a synopsis you would create a broader proposal, a separate page or two that explains a bit about the book. There are no hard and fast rules about how this should be formatted but I would suggest it needs to contain the following:

Book Summary. A paragraph or two that simply and concisely explains the concept of the book. If it is a history book, talk about which period and subjects it covers. With a biography of a famous person, explain who that person is and what their achievements are. If you have written a science book, outline the key themes and arguments. You get the idea. This is a taster of what the finished book will contain.

Book Detail. Having whetted their appetite with the summary, you can go into a bit more detail here. Perhaps 500-1000 words that expand upon the summary and explain the book. It works a bit like a synopsis, but as most non-fiction books do not have a strict plot, as such, you don't need to walk us through the entire 'story' from start to finish. Summarise the book's contents so that the recipient has a clear picture of what you are trying to do.

The Market. Although the agent or publisher does not expect you to be a marketing expert, they will consider it a plus if you have an understanding of the potential audience for your book. If you have written that book on Victorian architecture I mentioned above, then some stats about how many other people are interested in the subject would help – a Facebook group with a million members, a monthly magazine with 50,000 subscribers, that sort of thing. Also, some awareness of previous books on similar subjects would be good.

Biography. Time to say a little bit about yourself but focusing on your qualifications and why you are the person to write this book. If you are the country's leading expert on your subject, make that clear. If you have been given access to rare archives, mention it. And, obviously, details of any previous books you have written would help your case.

Chapter Breakdown

As mentioned earlier, many non-fiction books are pitched to, and signed up by, agents and publishers before they are written. In these cases, for obvious reasons, you can't really provide sample chapters so a chapter breakdown is usually expected instead.

Very simply this is a list of your planned chapters, in order, with a few lines of summary for each. At the end of the day, it will take the agent through your concept of the book and give them a clear idea of what you have in mind.

For example:

Introduction

A short introduction outlining the importance of Victorian architecture, how it influenced building design for many years and why a new study is needed.

Chapter One

A brief history of roof tiles and how they were used by 19th century architects in domestic and commercial buildings.

Chapter Two

A look at the revolution in doorsteps and doorstep-making technology in the 1870s. Includes never-before-seen details of the manufacturing process.

OK, so I am making this nonsense up, but I am sure you get the idea. More than three or four sentences for each summary is probably pushing it.

Although a set of completed chapters is not expected, if you are able to include some sample writing, perhaps just one draft chapter, it would help. An agent might love your proposal and love the sound of your book but simply not engage with your writing, in which case they are not the agent for you. Or, to flip that, they might not be totally convinced by your proposal but love your writing style and that alone may make them want to work with you.

A final non-fiction book submission would ideally include the proposal, chapter breakdown and sample writing as one document – the fewer attachments the better – but, as always, check the guidelines first.

Follow Up

Did I say writing the synopsis was the most difficult part of the submissions process? I was lying. Waiting for a response is the most difficult part. Now would be a good time to take up a new hobby or redecorate the spare room. Anything to take your mind off the fact that your much-loved creation is now in the hands of someone who could make or break it.

Leave it two months before chasing. In the short term, your submission may well be greeted by a deafening silence. Do not be tempted to check in or chase up until a couple of months have passed. If you attempt to chase earlier than this you will just come across as impatient and annoying. Agents and editors have lots of stuff to read. Agents, in particular, spend the bulk of their days reading submissions. It can take some time to get round to yours. Most will respond before too long, and they do not expect you to hang around forever. A polite email asking if they are still interested after two to four months will do the job. If you do not hear back after that then it is fair to move on.

Consider time of year. The London Book Fair in April and Frankfurt Book Fair in October keep agents extremely busy with lots of preparation and follow-up involved. If you have sent something in March or September then perhaps be prepared to wait a bit longer for a reply. August and January can also be quiet times with lots of agents buggering off to their gîtes in France or family piles in the Cotswolds. What's the US equivalent? The Hamptons?

Take rejection with good grace. Every agent and publisher has horror stories about authors who got nasty/went a bit doolally/turned into an arsehole when receiving a rejection. If you receive a standard stock rejection, just accept it as one of those things that happens and move on. If you receive some feedback, but your book is still rejected, be grateful and take the feedback on board. Do not get back in touch for more clarification, to complain that you have been unfairly treated, to bitch about the agent etc.

Do not resend unless invited. Even if you have received some helpful feedback it is not the done thing to resubmit the same book to an agent after rejection. If an agent wants you to do some work on your book and then resend it they will make that very clear.

Move on to the next name on your list. When you receive a rejection from one agent, you can then send your book to another. If you are working in groups of five or six then select the next in line, repeat the whole research process for them and then send your work.

* * *

Success

Let's be optimistic for a moment. Let's forget the odds that are stacked against you, and the rejection emails sitting in your inbox, and assume that an agent likes your submission and wants to read more. What happens next?

Well, first up, of course, you need to have something else to give them to read, especially in the case of fiction. I know of many cases where a writer has managed to get over the first hurdle, have their full manuscript called in, only to confess that the rest of the novel isn't quite ready, or isn't even finished. I am sure there are things that would piss off an agent more than this, but there won't be many.

You will almost certainly be asked to send in the full manuscript. If the agent, or publisher, has any specific guidelines they will make them clear in their request. By now you should know how I feel about guidelines. Just follow them. If there are no guidelines offered then don't bother the agent with lots of follow up questions, just make sure the manuscript is formatted in the same style as your submission and get ready to send it.

With non-fiction, the next steps will depend on the status of the manuscript. If the manuscript is complete then all of the above remains relevant.

If your non-fiction book is incomplete, and you made that clear in your submission, then the agent is almost certainly going to be more specific in their request. Pay attention to what they ask for. They may want more sample material, or a more detailed chapter breakdown, or they want to chat about the book over the phone or in person. As always, it pays to simply do as they ask and not overcomplicate things.

Having spent so much time perfecting your submission it makes sense to spend some time checking over your manuscript before sending it off. Now is not the time to rewrite big chunks of it, even if you are suddenly experiencing a crisis of confidence, but it would be good to read through the whole thing once more to mop up any typos or fix any little glitches. It doesn't have to be absolutely perfect but let's make it as good as possible before sending it off.

Once you send it off then yet another waiting game begins.

If an agent has called in your manuscript then the chances are they will be reading it themselves and, given all the other stuff they are working on, this will take time. How long does it take you to read a book? A couple of days? A week? Two? Well, an agent could well take that long, or even more, to finish reading yours. We hope, of course, that they drop everything as soon as your manuscript arrives, and that might happen, but let's be realistic.

When the response does come, it could take one of several forms.

Rejection. The agent may decide, having read the whole book, that it is not for them. This does not mean that the book isn't publishable and that all your hopes are dashed, just that this particular agent didn't feel they could add anything to the package, or find the right home, or didn't quite love it enough to want to represent it. You would hope that a rejection at this stage will include some specific feedback but that won't always happen. If it does, embrace it and digest it, it should be very useful as you dust yourself off and go back out there with your book.

Rewrite. The agent may get back to you with suggestions or requests for rewrites. This is a very good sign as it means they a clearly interested in the book, but it does not constitute an offer. Many authors have rewritten their entire books, sometimes a number of times, only for an agent to ultimately decide not to take it on, but we are being optimistic for a while, so let's move on.

Meeting. Most agents will want to meet with an author before offering to represent them and this is a process that has benefits for both parties. The agent will be your professional partner in your writing career and it is important that the two of you click. You don't have to be best mates (although that does happen sometimes) but you do need to get on and respect each other.

Of course, a meeting isn't always possible but a phone call, or Skype session, is a reasonable alternative. Either way, you need to have a good natter about you, your work and both your plans for it.

At this stage, the relationship takes an interesting turn. Having spent the last several weeks and months trying to convince an agent to take on your work, you now have an agent trying to convince you to employ them to represent you. Don't let all the power go to your head but, you know, allow yourself a little smile.

I won't linger any more on this, this is a book about perfecting your submission and we are in danger of moving all the way to publication, but I wanted to at least address this stage of the process for you.

* * *

Some Positive Thoughts

I realise I have spent much of this book saying 'Do this' and 'Don't do that' and generally telling you how hard this whole process would be so, just before we come to the end of this short book I want to share some positive thoughts.

Every time an agent or publisher opens up a submission they want it to be amazing. They want it to be something they fall in love with, that they cannot put down. They want to get to the end of the sample chapters with an urge to read more. They really do want you to succeed. And therefore they'll be quite forgiving.

We do not expect your submission to be perfect. We'll overlook little errors and issues, especially if your story is strong and compelling. We are, in the main, quite nice people. Honest.

But we do get sent a lot of things to read, a lot of things to consider, and over the years we have developed certain skills, certain shorthand, for identifying manuscripts that are, in all probability, not for us. I just don't want you to fall foul of any of that.

Also, don't view every rejection as a negative thing. You deserve to be represented or published by someone who loves your work. If someone reads your submission and is lukewarm about it, it is probably a good thing that they don't sign you up – you want someone to champion your writing, to shout about how great you are – and you definitely don't want to be involved with someone who doesn't like your work at all and is only in it for the money. The submissions process is about finding someone who is write for you and your book, it is unlikely to happen immediately.

Just remember, we really do want your book to be wonderful. There is nothing we like more.

* * *

Conclusion

So there you have it, my advice on how to perfect your submission. I cannot guarantee you will get your book published – it could be terrible for all I know – but, if you follow these guidelines, you will have avoided the mistakes that other aspiring writers make on a regular basis, you will have pulled together a strong submission package and you will have given yourself, and your work, the best chance to take the next steps to publication.

If you do get published, what lies ahead of you is every bit as scary, daunting and unpredictable as the submissions process has been. You and your work will be pulled apart, scrutinised, criticised and reviewed, and sometimes that won't be a very pleasant experience, but if your book ends up in the hands of one reader, just one reader, for whom it really means something, then it will have all been worth it.

Good luck. You're going to need it.

FAQs

I hope I have covered everything you need to know, albeit in a general fashion, in this book, but here are some questions that I, and agents, get asked a lot along with some questions I have been asked by readers who have bought this book in the past.

Q: I have previously self-published my work, will it count against me?

A: This may have been the case a few years ago but there have been so many self-published successes of late that very few agents will be bothered by a self-publishing past. It may even be seen as a bonus, especially if you managed to sell a fair number of copies.

In general, agents won't consider books that you have already self-published, unless they have sold bucketloads, so best not to submit something that has such a background unless the agent has specifically said it is OK.

Suffice to say, any agent who would be bothered by a self-published author isn't the agent for you.

Q: I cannot possibly get my synopsis on to one page, can I submit a two- to three-page synopsis instead?

A: Firstly, you are not trying hard enough. Any book can by summarised in one page if you really focus. But, for the sake of argument, let's assume it is completely impossible to keep the synopsis to just the one page.

If the guidelines for your chosen agent or publisher has a word-count or page-length requirement, and you are currently over that limit — tough luck. Ignore those guidelines at your peril.

If, and some do, your chosen recipient does not have such guidelines then you can, by all means, give it a go. But I have yet to meet an agent or publisher whose heart doesn't sink when they see a three-page synopsis. Why put them through that?

Q: I am not sure what genre to classify my book as, what should I do?

A: Ask yourself this question: In which section of a bookshop do I want my book to be shelved? That's your genre. If you need to be more specific than just 'Fiction' then you could check out the Amazon category for books you feel are similar to yours and use that. Don't get too specific.'Fantasy Fiction' is fine, 'Historical Cyberpunk Romance' isn't a genre that many agents will be able to relate to.

Q: Should I outline the market for my book in my query letter?

A: Authors often do this, and there isn't any harm in it if the information is presented well, but if the agent or publisher hasn't asked for it then it isn't essential. Chances are the agent or publisher will know more about the market than you do anyway.

Q: In my cover letter, should I mention any workshops or creative writing classes I have attended?

A: That depends. If you are the graduate of a recognised creative writing degree course, or a well-known class or workshop, then by all means mention it. The same goes for awards. But little-known or obscure courses aren't really going to help your case all that much. They certainly won't make or break your submission.

Q: Do I need a brand and how much will it hamper me if I haven't got one?

A: I do get asked this a lot. If you have a strong brand, either as the owner of a website or a specialist in a certain field, then it is worth shouting about, and can be particularly useful for non-fiction projects, but it is by no means essential. It can help but the lack of one won't hurt you.

Q: If my work is experimental, plays with genre tropes or otherwise proves unexpected or even controversial, should I warn in advance or let them find out for themselves?

A: If you have followed the guidelines in this book correctly then you should know not to hide anything from the agent or publisher. Tell them what they are getting, plain and simple.

Q: Is it OK to resubmit a manuscript to an agent once I have reworked it?

A: Unless you have been requested to resubmit it then no.

Q: I have received a rejection but I have some follow up questions, is it OK to drop the agent an email?

A: No. If the agent wants you to get in touch they will invite you to do so.

Q: I feel I have been unfairly treated, how do I go about complaining?

A: Grow up. If you receive a rejection, take it with good grace and move on.

Q: My book has a major plot twist at the end and I don't want to spoil this in my synopsis, is it OK to keep it secret?

A: No, it isn't. Bear in mind that you are probably only sending a synopsis and a few chapters, so the recipient will have no idea what your twist is even if they read all the material you have sent. If your twist is so bloody great then tell us about it.

Q: I am worried about sending my work out to an agent in case they steal my idea, how can I protect myself against this?

A: Relax. If you are sending your work to a reputable agent or publisher then this really is not going to happen. The chances that your work is so amazing, so incredible, that a publishing professional is going to risk their careers by nicking it are pretty much zero. Simply by writing the work in the first place you have automatic copyright, and this is solid protection.

Q: I have found an agent who wants to read my work but they charge a small administration fee, should I pay it?

A: This one is easy. Never pay anyone a fee when submitting your work. These are always scams. No reputable agent or publisher will charge you anything to read your submission.

Q: Should I pay an editor to work on my manuscript before I submit it?

A: That is up to you. If you have had quality feedback from early readers and are confident that your book is as good as it can be, then you might as well submit it. However, if you have some nagging doubts about certain aspects – plot, character, dialogue or whatever – then it may well help to have a publishing professional look over it. It is unlikely that you'll need a line-by-line edit, just an editorial assessment should be enough. This is where an editor reads your book and write up a report on issues, areas of concern, things that could be improved and so on. It is a service I provide in my day job as a freelance editor and work on many such assessments every year.

Q: I have an excellent cover design for my book already,

is it OK to include that with my submission? I want the agent to have an idea of how I want the book to look.

Are you a professional cover designer? I am guessing not. In which case, do not send a cover design. It is never a good idea and can send out the wrong signals. Whenever an author has done this to me the cover has been crap, 100% of the time.

Q: How should I address the agent in my query letter?

This may be the question I get asked more than any other. If you are of a certain age, and I won't be specific so as not to embarrass anyone, then you will have been taught at school the importance of correct use of titles – Mrs, Mr, Dr, Sir, Madam, Ms, Miss and so on – and it can be really hard to let them go, but I am going to ask you to do just that.

If the recipient is a man, then the form of address is easy. Our patriarchal society has decreed that there is generally only one form of address needed for a man, and that is Mr. If I receive a submission addressed to Mr Pack then I don't bat an eyelid. All fine.

But with women it becomes more difficult. We have Mrs, Miss and Ms available to us here. Which one to use? Lord knows, quite frankly. Firstly, either of the first two could be technically incorrect depending on the marital status of the recipient, let alone their personal preference. So, many feel that Ms is a safe option, but then I know loads of women who hate being called Ms.

And what is more, we live in a world where, thankfully, people feel more comfortable with gender fluidity and there is no guarantee that the recipient will identify as male or female anyway.

My suggestion? Just use the first name. Dear Scott works absolutely fine. Now, I know there are some people who just cannot bring themselves to address a stranger by their first name but it probably is the safest option.

Appendix 1: Query Letter Template

Here is a template for a query letter, using a completely made-up novel. Feel free to copy it and adapt it for your own use. Please note, if sending to a publisher rather than an agent then the opening line would need to change to something like: I am submitting for your consideration my crime novel...

Dear Scott,

I am seeking representation for my crime novel, *Where Evil Remains*, which is complete at 85,000 words.

I wanted to submit my work to you after seeing you speak at the Winchester Writers' Festival last year. You spoke about the sort of books you were looking for and I felt my novel, which I was in the process of re-drafting at that stage, might just fit the bill.

Where Evil Remains is a gritty crime novel set in the East End of London. A Land Rover is found parked on some waste ground near to Mile End tube station. The driver and passenger, both men in smart suits, have been killed by single gunshot wounds to the head. When D.I. Susie Baines recognises them as local drug dealers she realises that the list of suspects will be very long indeed. What she doesn't know is that the culprit is a lot closer to home than she thinks.

I hope that fans of authors such as Peter James and Nicci French would like my book, and early readers have made those sort of comparisons, which is most flattering.

I have been a police community support officer serving in the East End for the past decade and, although my book is very much a work of fiction, I have used my experience, and the many stories I have heard from my colleagues in the full-time force, to inform my writing.

I attach a synopsis and the first three chapters of the book, as requested in your submission guidelines. If you would like to read the full novel I would be delighted to send it over to you.

Thanks for taking the time to read my work.

Kind regards,

Scott Pack

Appendix 2: Contact Details

I offer freelance editorial services including checking your submissions package, an editorial review of your manuscript and a full structural edit.

I can also present *How to Perfect Your Submission* as a dynamic interactive workshop, complete with swearing, to your festival or writing group. And, yes, I can do it via Zoom or any other video conferencing software.

Feel free to drop me a line for more details.

Email: thatscottpack@gmail.com

Twitter: @meandmybigmouth

Reedsy: reedsy.com/scottpack

Acknowledgements

Thanks to everyone who has attended my Guardian Masterclasses over the years, as well as those who sat through somewhat shorter versions of the same presentations at literary and writers' festivals up and down the land. Your questions and feedback have helped to inform this ebook.

A one-man standing ovation to my beta readers: Sarah O'Connor, Jackie Bates, Sian Meades and James Burt. I hope your submissions will be snapped up by agents the moment you send them out.

Ifan Bates did the cover of this ebook, for which I am most grateful.

My friend, business partner and favourite pedant, Kat Stephen, read through this lots of times, offered suggestions and then proof read the thing. I love her. She's ace.